Silver Lake Sampler

Marjorie Turner Hollman

Adapted excerpt from <u>Splitting Seeds: Songs and Stories from the Threshing Floor</u> © 2012 by Mary Ellen Potter. Used with permission.

Interviews with George and Kathryn Whiting first published in the Bellingham Bulletin. (bellinghambulletin.com) Used with permission.

Silver Lake Sampler
Collection of Personal History excerpts
1.Non-Fiction 2. Memoir 3. Personal History 4. Story Collection

MarjorieTurner.com
Bellingham, MA 02019

What Clients Have to Say

Working with Marjorie was like talking with someone who listened to my heart, rather than telling me what to say. *Mary Potter, Walpole, MA*

Personal histories are so powerful. Marjorie asked me the right questions about my uncle, who died a hero's death in WWII. It was wonderful to see her interest, and to share with her my experience of learning about him. She took the essence of my uncle's story and brought it to life in her writing. *Linda Hardin, Franklin, MA*

Marjorie knows how to craft compelling and engaging written stories. The personal history she produced with our dad was a wonderful gift to me, and to our entire family as well. *Mary Glen Chitty, Somerville, MA*

Because Marjorie helped our dad put together his personal history, I heard stories that I had forgotten, things that happened when I was a kid. This gave me a chance to talk with Dad and learn more about what happened. Reading his stories has allowed my kids to get to know and appreciate their grandparents in a way they would have otherwise never had a chance to. It has prompted my kids to ask me questions about my own experiences with Dad, which has helped us feel closer as a family. *Rob Kuhl, Jacksonville, FL*

My husband and I both enjoyed our visits when Marjorie interviewed us. She was nice, humble, and easy to talk to. *Kathryn Whiting, Bellingham, MA*

Choosing to Share

Who would want to hear my stories? I'm not famous. Writing a memoir is just for famous people. I've never done anything interesting. I'll write down my stories someday when I get the time.

Any other excuses? Now ask yourself: what would it mean to have stories or letters that your grandparents wrote? Would you think they were unimportant because your grandparents weren't famous?

Think about your box of unlabeled photos. Will anyone know who is in those pictures if you don't organize and label them? The same holds true for your stories. Unless you've documented them, your stories will be lost.

In the process of working with a personal historian, forgotten stories bubble to the surface. Experiences from long ago come back, insisting that they too be included in the book—your book, your story.

Many people have written memoirs on their own; but, for most of us, our life stories are like that musty box of photos, forgotten, and fading with time. Working with a personal historian will ensure that the job of documenting your stories gets done.

This booklet contains stories people have shared with me, simple tales that make a life. I hope you enjoy reading them as much as I enjoyed hearing them and then crafting these stories into captivating and meaningful narrative. Every story included here is a gift from the heart.

Marjorie Turner Hollman

Life in the Tropics: Miami in the Late 1930's

My dad Don Kuhl was born in Minnesota, but his family left there when Don was fourteen, hoping to find a place where his father could live in less pain, despite his arthritis. The family finally settled in Miami, Florida. Don died recently at home in his favorite green chair. He was always my best listener, and I miss him.

The following are excerpts from Don's memoir, From Minnesota to Florida: Finding a Place in the Sun–Kuhl Family Stories. I've also included a story at the end that Don's sister Betty Kuhl Nickinson shared with me after Don's memoir went to press. Her added story gives me a hint of where our family's sense of humor came from.

Don: When I was in high school, I enjoyed skin diving in Miami with my friends. We couldn't go out and buy commercial masks or flippers then; we had to make them ourselves. The fellows I spent time with right after high school had made masks for themselves, and they helped me make one out of red rubber. I cut it to fit around my face, cut a piece of glass to fit my face, then used metal to hold it together. They also helped me make a spear gun.

They never let someone new to the group take a loaded gun the first several times they went out. They wanted to make sure you knew what you were doing. For the spear gun, we used a ten-foot galvanized rod, cut it in half, made a blunt end, drilled a hole and put a barb in it. That's what we speared the fish with. We used inner tubes from bike tires for slings to fire the gun. The spear point had to be blunt. When the tip hit a fish scale, it would stop; then the barb would slide along the fish scale, get between the scales and pierce the fish.

One time I went out fishing in the evening with my friends Lloyd and Ethel. We went over to the new causeway over Biscayne Bay in Miami and as I often did, all I took was my shrimp nets and a bucket. The tide had just changed to dead low when we got there, and it was full of weeds, so I wandered along another bank, wading and looking around. I got the biggest kick out of that, just walking in water maybe knee deep and seeing what was going on. I netted a little mullet, a shiner, and one little shrimp and just had the biggest time. I gave them to Lloyd and wandered around watching the people on the beach.

I stopped to talk with a man and his wife—he was from Cuba, and his wife was from Spain. They had just a few crabs, a hermit crab and a squid. The man explained all about the squid to me. I'd never seen one before. It was all brown when they first brought it up and later lost all of its color and was transparent. We could see its stomach working right through its side and it had what appeared to be vents along each side. It shut the vents and seemed to blow air out of them. It was a very odd fish—I figured it must have been jet-propelled.

I'll never forget the day a school of fish went by as I was swimming underwater, beneath a jetty in South Miami. I had taken a loaded spear gun in my hand when a solid wall of red snappers came by. Those snappers kept swimming past me until they finally rounded the corner of the jetty and disappeared. There were so many fish that I couldn't see through them. It was the most beautiful, calm and peaceful experience I've had in my whole life. I could no more shoot those fish than I could have shot anything.

I have no idea how long it took for the fish to pass by, but I was limited in time, since I was perhaps twelve feet under water. Those fish went by me unperturbed. How fast they swam, I don't know. They were all snappers, but there were great big ones and little ones.

The mature fish were bigger than I'd ever seen. They were beautiful, very colorful.

The fish finally all swam off so I could get to the surface and start breathing again, but while they were going by I couldn't leave: I was spellbound. I would love to have on a wall a picture comparable to what I saw, but that's impossible—I'd run out of house.

Betty: One day Don and his friends were in our kitchen in Miami getting ready to cook up some fish they'd caught. Don's friend Tony had put some oil in a frying pan. He stood in the kitchen trying to figure out which burner to put the pan on, but he didn't realize that the pan's handle was loose. "Mrs. Kuhl, where should I put this?" he asked our mom. Just then the handle turned and the oil went all over the floor. Mom looked at him and without missing a beat replied, "Oh, just put it on the floor, Tony."

Angel in Disguise

Mary Potter, of Walpole, Massachusetts, created a series of drawings and poems about twenty-five years ago. I worked with her recently to craft a narrative reflecting her experiences before and since that time, which we interwove with her artwork and poetry. Her book, <u>Splitting Seeds: Songs and Stories from the Threshing Floor</u> is the result of our work together. This adapted excerpt relates the story of her father's beginnings and the woman who taught him about love.

Mary: My dad's mother died when Dad was two days old. His mother was very young, just nineteen, and his father was twenty— they were just kids themselves. Dad was at the hospital and wouldn't take any formula. When Mary Ellen Webster, the family's housekeeper, heard this, she marched down to Norwood Hospital and demanded the baby. She carried Dad home under her arm like a little football and got him to eat by putting a little brandy in his milk.

Mary Ellen made sure Dad had special things. He told us stories of how much he adored Mary Ellen, and how she and others always looked out for him. This angel raised Dad until he was eight years old, when she died. But she urged her sixteen-year-old daughter, Auntie Bea, to take care of him.

I asked Dad once if he felt angry that he'd lived in so many different places when he was growing up. He said, "No, because everywhere I went somebody loved me. I always felt that, so there was no need to be angry with anybody." It was a wonderful lesson for me. I thought that if my dad could forgive that, then forgiveness must be a wonderful thing.

This was a gift that he passed on to me. It enabled him to be an incredible father. He got up in the middle of the night when my mother pretended she was asleep. He fed us and loved us. I was attached to his hip most of the time and mimicked what he did, sitting and crossing my arms the same way as he did.

When I was older, he told me, "If Mary Ellen Webster had lived, she'd be your grandmother because that was the mother I knew. I heard stories about my mother, that she was beautiful, but Mary Ellen Webster loved me." So I was named Mary Ellen, after her. She saw a child in need and decided that she was going to take care of him, and that was that.

Learning to Ride

Bill Hollman now lives in Newton, Massachusetts, but grew up in Brookline, Massachusetts during the Depression. Bill was hit by a car when he was five, and carried the effects of that accident for years. His parents owned a small grocery store. This is a story he shared about a gift he received from a young man who worked at his parent's store.

Bill: We had an employee who was in his late teens, a young man named Patrick. I spent a lot of time talking with him down at the store. He was very personable and friendly, but of course very different from my Jewish family members. He was Italian and Catholic. He got me something I'd always wanted, which was a B-B gun. I loved the idea of being able to shoot a rifle, because I couldn't run very well. I used the gun, but one day it "disappeared." My mother thought it was too dangerous, and it was, but taking it away from me made me very upset.

Patrick gave me another gift, however. He had a bicycle, which he used to deliver groceries to our customers. I always wanted to learn how to ride a two-wheeler. There was a dead-end street two blocks from where my father's store was, behind Temple Israel. One day Patrick took me to that dead-end street with his bike and told me, "I'll hold the seat; you pedal and steer." And he did. I said to him, "Gee, this is great." Then I realized that nobody had answered me. I'd gone down the street balancing myself on the bike and hadn't realized it. As soon as I figured this out I came to a sudden halt. But Patrick came right over and said, "Get on and I'll help you start." Lo and behold, I was riding a bike!

My parents then got me a Columbia one-speed bike and that bike took me everywhere: to the train yard, to Braves Field at Boston University, down the Riverway, all kinds I places that I could now travel. I wasn't very athletic because I'd worn a brace for several years. I climbed trees and ran, but not like other kids. I had no pain, and my hip had regrown, but I never had the range of physical activities of other kids. I did wander up and down the Riverway and crossed the Boston and Albany railroad tracks to get to the Riverway through a hole in the fence.

I rode that bike to watch the ball games at Braves Field, and I guess I enjoyed going to ball games later in life. I may have taken my children to ball games, but it certainly wasn't often and it wasn't a passion for me the way sports are a passion for many young people. Part of that came from not being very athletic, given my accident. I couldn't run around when the other kids did—but I could climb trees, and ride a bike!

Surviving the 1938 Hurricane and Rebuilding

George and Kathryn Whiting still live in the house where George was born in South Bellingham, Massachusetts. George recently talked with me about the destruction of his family's chicken farm by the '38 hurricane.

George: Back then we didn't have weather reports like we do now. We heard radio reports of a storm that was coming up the coast, but that's all. We'd never heard of hurricanes. My cousins who were visiting wanted to see the ocean when it was rough, so my father drove them down to Narragansett Pier. When the surf became violent they left, and had to detour over downed trees and wires to get home.

When they got back, my father headed to the chicken coops. We had a chicken farm, right here behind our house. My father found my older brother and me down in one of the buildings.

The wind was so strong it kept lifting the sill off the foundation. We had sledge hammers, and kept pounding the sill back down. My father said, "Get out of that building. This coop is going to go!" We ran out, and he had just let go of the door latch when the building let go and blew up into the air. We walked over the wreckage to get back to the house.

My uncle had gone to use the outhouse when they got back from the beach. When the roof of that chicken coop flew off, it slammed right against the outhouse. My poor uncle came out of there looking like a ghost!

At that time we were raising about 15,000 chickens. We lost hundreds, thousands of chickens in that storm. Only one building and our house were still standing afterwards.

Over the next few weeks my father and some fellows who worked here framed new buildings during the week. Each Sunday neighbors, friends, maybe fifteen people came over to help get another chicken coop back up. We reused the wreckage from the old coops. I'd lay out the boards and drive the nails out. Then I'd straighten them and fill a whole bucket with the nails I salvaged. Any board that was good enough went back on a building.

To keep the business going my father had to go to other farms in the area to get eggs for our customers. We weighed and cleaned 300 dozen eggs a day. Since we were without electricity for three weeks after that storm, all the work we'd automated to process the eggs had to be done by hand. Somehow, we built the business back up.

Never Look for Excuses

Kathryn Whiting moved to Bellingham, Massachusetts from New York City when she was six months old. Both Kathryn and her husband, George, grew up in Bellingham, met in high school, married and raised a family there. Kathryn spoke to me about her mother, widowed when Kathryn was six years old, and the challenging life her mother led as a single parent.

Kathryn: My father had a successful upholstery business in New York City and met my mother there, where she was a registered nurse. My father was from the Boston area and took sick when I was just a tiny baby. Because of his illness he lost his business in New York. They came back here to Bellingham when I was six months old.

My father died when I was six years old, and there was no such thing as any kind of help in those days. There was only the poor farm, located on Farm Street in Bellingham, which my husband George's grandfather ran for a time. The farm is no longer there. We lived in a house on Taunton Street—one of only two houses on the street back then. We had a miniature poultry farm and raised a few vegetables and the like.

Because my mother was a nurse, the City of Boston allowed her to have many, many more foster children than the law allowed. At times we had as many as fourteen to sixteen children. Other families in town took in foster children as well. Ida Hood Parker's family took in girls, and her grandfather's family across the street took in boys to work on their farm.

We had a goat that was like a puppy to us. It was allowed in the house when the state inspectors weren't there. But one day the state inspector came by and one of the young children let the goat into the house. Up the stair the goat came, to where the inspector was looking at the bedrooms. My mother put on an act that this was the first time the goat had come into the house. "Heavens, what's that goat doing in the house?" she said. And all the children went along with her.

My mother treated me exactly the way these foster children were treated, which was the right way to go. I was never put on a pedestal. After breakfast one morning I went upstairs and found one of the little girls, Anna, crying. I asked her, "Anna, why aren't you out with us? What's the matter?"

"What's the matter with you?" she answered. "When you get told what I was told this morning, you'll be crying too. They're coming to take me away tomorrow." You see, the authorities never let any of those children stay in one place too long. They didn't want the children to get too attached. Anna warned me, "When they tell you that, you'll be crying too. This was the best home I ever had." Anna didn't realize that her foster mother was my mother. You see, my mother was very fair—when I deserved discipline, I got it.

My mother remarried when I was eight and my step-father was a wonderful man. My mother died just before the town's previous centennial and we had an open house planned. Everyone was invited to come tour our house. Boy, I wasn't up to that, but my son said, "Come on Mom, that isn't the way you brought us up," and he was right. I always said to them, "Mom always said, 'You don't say I can't.'" I knew that if anyone had a reason to say "I can't," she did, but she never looked for excuses.

What is a Personal History?

Personal histories come in many flavors. Some people choose to create a story with a topical focus. Others may wish to tell their story using mostly photographs. It can be a simple recounting of one person's story, or two or more family members may contribute to a family's personal history.

Each family is different, and has different goals in passing on their stories. Every project is unique, and is created with regular collaboration between the person(s) sharing the stories and the personal historian. The common thread is that the stories are written in the storyteller's own voice, first person.

When a person tells me her stories, I regard this sharing as a sacred trust. Only the stories the client wishes to pass on are included in the final publication. It is my privilege to be entrusted with these stories and to participate in a process that results in books that are filled with life.

I welcome your inquiries. My contact information:

Marjorie Turner Hollman
Bellingham, MA 02019
508-883-3443
Marjorie@marjorieturner.com
marjorieturner.com

Make Your Story into a Book

Documenting your stories is the first step. Making your stories accessible to others is an additional process that can be as simple as typing and printing out a single manuscript, or as complex as hiring a book designer, cover designer, and arranging a contract with a printer.

Available options for publishing your book include using either off-set, for a large number of copies, or Print on Demand (POD) for fewer copies. You might choose hard-cover or paperback books. Perhaps you want to include color photographs, incorporate color into the page design, or use a simple black-and-white format. All these choices and more affect the cost of publication.

POD allows you to order one or many copies, and makes ordering additional copies easy. This may be the most affordable option for sharing your personal history with family and friends.

We are happy to explain the process and work with you to help produce the personal history you have in mind. Understanding what is involved in producing a publication can help you choose which options work best for you and your family. Silver Lake Publications has experience producing books you can be proud to share with your family and friends.

Marjorie Turner Hollman
Bellingham, MA 02019
508-883-3443
Marjorie@marjorieturner.com
marjorieturner.com